You Can Volunteer!

CIVIC VIRTUES

Spencer Toole

CIVICS FOR THE REAL WORLD™

Rosen Classroom™

You can help people in your community. You can volunteer!

Volunteering is when you help your community for no pay. It's a nice thing to do.

You can volunteer at a soup kitchen. You can help feed hungry people in need.

You can volunteer to sort clothes. You can help people in need stay warm.

You can volunteer with kids.
You can help them learn
to read books.

You can volunteer with old people. You can play a card game with them.

You can volunteer to help your neighbors. You can use a shovel to clear their steps.

You can volunteer at a town park. You can clean up trash.

You can volunteer to walk dogs. Animals need help, too!

Volunteering makes your community a better place. This is good for everyone!

WORDS TO KNOW

card game

community

shovel

trash